D0839455

Books by Erin C. Mahoney

Girl Power Guidebook: The Program, Strategies, and Insights that Transform and Empower Girls

Girl Power Journal: Be Strong. Be Smart. Be Amazing!

Positive

Vibes

for Women

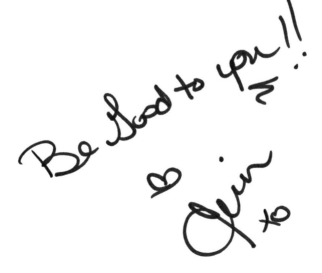

Be Good to you!!
♡ Jim
xo

Positive Vibes

for Women

Erin C. Mahoney
Founder of Girl Power Go

Girl Power Go

For Danielle

"And the day came when the risk to remain tight in a bud was more painful than the risk it took to blossom."

— Anaïs Nin

About the Quote

I love the quote on the previous page.

I have it on a bracelet I keep on my wrist, where I see it every day.

It's what happened to me.

We stand in a position of safety for so long before we come to a crossroads, and I finally allowed myself to blossom.

In This Book

———— ℘ ————

Alice laughed: "There's no use trying," she said; "one can't believe impossible things."

"I daresay you haven't had much practice," said the Queen. "When I was younger, I always did it for half an hour a day. Why, sometimes I've believed as many as six impossible things before breakfast."

—from *Alice in Wonderland*
by Lewis Carroll

Introduction: The Power of You

——— ℰℴ ———

Are you missing your life? And if you *are* missing your life, when do you gain that awareness? I was missing mine. I was working *so hard*, until I realized I was missing everything that was most important to me. My kids, for example, were growing really fast. There was a time before I was doing Girl Power full time, when I had personal training clients, nutrition clients, runners I trained, and I was working around the clock. I was getting up early to see clients, working all day, then going back to work after putting my kids to bed.

We had a really nice ritual where at bedtime we did prayers and I would tuck them in. Over time it seemed my husband was doing more of the evening prayers. Each night he would come downstairs to my office and tell me, "They're tucked." That was my cue to head upstairs. I would give them kisses and one last "tuck" before they drifted off to sleep.

"Come up, Mom! We're ready!" they'd say.

"Okay," I'd say, "just a second," and I would get caught up working again. At times I would realize that I lost track of time and race upstairs only to see that they fell asleep waiting for me. I had all of this guilt about it—*Oh my gosh, why didn't I go up sooner?* I had missed the moment, and I would tell myself I suck. Yet there I was, night after night getting distracted by my work, stressed about all I had to do for the next day or the coming week—*Just one more email to answer, just one more client to check in with.*

And then one night my youngest son called out for my *husband* instead of me. No more "Mom, we're ready to do prayers" or "Mom, are you coming up to tuck us in?" It was just, "Dad, we're ready to do prayers!" They knew before I did that I wasn't coming up to tuck them in. I was missing the most important moments of my life.

The good news is, I'm not missing them anymore!

It still makes me sad to think about that night but the lesson I learned and the work I did to *get present* after that moment changed my life!

So I thought, *What is preventing me from slamming this laptop shut, and just being done for the day? It's eight-thirty at night, I started at five o'clock in the morning!*

That was a huge ah-ha moment.

Today I ask the ladies that I work with to look for moments where they might be feeling like *I want to be somewhere else, or doing something else*, and ask themselves, "Why? What is so important? Why are you missing your life?"

For me back then, I was working in a multi-level marketing business on top of everything else I was trying to do in my fitness business and I always felt like *I'll just put in one more order. That will make me and my family a few more bucks. I'll just chase the hustle a little longer and then I will feel like I am worthy and successful.*

But when my kids didn't call for me that night, I realized that my entire focus was off and I could not continue missing the most meaningful moments in my life.

I know I am *not* the only person something like that has happened to. It doesn't mean we suck, it just means we have to readjust. I needed to shift, I needed to look at what was most important for me. Today, too many people are rushing from one thing to another and as a result they don't feel like they are good at *anything*. If you live your life like that, you're never going to get to where you really want to be. And at the same time, life doesn't have to be as hard as some people make it.

Every human being has those moments where we feel like, "My God, I wish I would have done it differently," but it's *never too late* to do it differently, as long as you're here, as long as you are showing up, you are powerful. I hate to be the one to break it to you, but it's true. You have no more excuses. You can choose, and you can be the *you* that you have always wanted to be, and more. You can be *that you* with happiness, fulfillment, and serving others. And you can be that you *today*.

My vision was to create a sweet little book women can throw in their purses or leave on the bedside table, and remind themselves *they are awesome*. It's about getting women to think in a more loving and caring way about themselves. I hope when you put this book down you can say, "Oh my gosh, I feel so much better!" Or you realize, "I do that to myself all of the time—*why?*"

I realized years ago after much of my own personal development work that I had the ability to make decisions from a *meaningful* place, that it's all about choices and owning them, and the sooner I started living that way the sooner I would be able to fully enjoy my life.

I decided that if I wanted to be at the hockey rink to see my kids play, then I no longer would get to tell myself that I should be working. I decided from that day forward, I would be truly *present*, both physically and emotionally. For those things most important to me, I would always do my best be *in the moment*. I didn't want to miss any more of my life, or theirs.

Along with it, I was going to give myself a break once in a while. I was going to take care of myself, too. Knowing that we live our lives at such a fast pace these days, is that easier said than done? Of course it is, but with practice every day you can get there. You can arrive in a place that feels meaningful and fulfilling without guilt or second-guessing. It's ongoing work you must do daily. You will need to sort out some things for yourself. Life changes, but with practice, self-compassion, and patience, *you stop missing your life.*

I am by no means a therapist but I have learned a thing or two about living my best life. I love research, learning from others, reading great books, and practicing positive, loving behavior. I create curriculum, programs, and workshops in the hopes of helping others realize their true potential while being present and loving themselves along the way.

But know that it's *work*. Acknowledge that it can be *hard* work. If you're willing to do the work, you can know that you *will* heal, you *will* feel better. Realize that so little is actually an emergency. We don't have to make every big decision about our lives in the fire of the moment. It's okay to take a few breaths and step back, to take a few days and figure out what's really important.

We can reach super-peaceful states but only when we put forth the effort with an open heart and an open mind. We must be willing to learn and make changes, no matter how scary that may seem. I want women to fall deeply in love with themselves. We can feel grounded, with the sun upon us, and free, like the woman on the cover of this book. We can focus on and show up for what's really important to us. It's all about the choices you make and how you decide to hold your energy.

On the pages that follow, I'm going to focus on those aspects of each of those *six powers* that seem to get lost in our busy days. There are a million books and articles about setting goals, so why don't all women do this perfectly? Where do we get hung up? After training and listening to thousands of women and journeying deep into my own heart for answers, these are the things women need to know to connect the dots of their lives. And when we have the dots connected, like a instrument that has had its cracks mended, we can play music without disharmony again, we can enjoy *positive vibes*, and we can share them with the world.

I want this book to help you, to open your heart, to open your mind to truly being yourself, to bequeath to you your birthright of these six powers, and to be in love with the moment.

That's power, and that's YOU.

"You deserve to be happy, you deserve to be joyful, you deserve to be celebrated. But in order to do that you must first fall madly in love with yourself."

—Lisa Nichols

{ 1 } The Power of Self-Love

———— &) ————

Part of finding balance includes always being kind and caring to yourself. The first step of self-love is acknowledging that you deserve to have it! Love and kindness are things that we all deserve and desire. All human beings want to feel loved. I'm not sure when or why, but somewhere along the line many of us feel as if we don't get to give ourselves compassion. Compassion is a word for a very positive emotion that has to do with being thoughtful and decent, caring, loving, and kind. So many women that I know have forgotten how to show themselves compassion at one time or another—myself included!

When I pull women together in a workshop, despite being in different careers, practicing different religions, being women with different ethnic backgrounds or family dynamics, at the root of it all, at the core, we're all the same—beautiful, powerful beings that want and need to be reminded of our value, worth, and how to practice loving ourselves.

And for me, I realized I cannot ask the women at my workshops to do something that I myself am not doing. It's amazing when you realize all the effort and practice that it takes to be truly in love with yourself. The important thing to know here is that self-love takes time—time to reflect and time to grow. Those are necessary parts of learning to love yourself.

Along my own personal journey, I was never slowing down, always juggling a thousand balls, because I was not completely comfortable in my own skin. I didn't really know it at the time and I certainly didn't want to admit it, but I was afraid—afraid if I slowed down I might have to actually see myself. It's only when you let yourself get quiet that you have an opportunity to look deep within yourself, from the inside out.

So I got quiet!

Years ago I became a certified yoga instructor, which sparked my interest in studying and learning meditation. I fell in love with meditation. I learned very quickly the value of slowing down. The study of meditation forced me to slow down and observe, and to be *present*. There are great gifts found in practicing things that slow you down but it takes practice. When you sit still long enough, you find balance. During quiet or "slowing down" times it's important to be loving and kind to yourself. It's a great act of self-love and self-care to speak to yourself with compassion and grace. It's okay and healing to say things that allow you to just *be*. Acknowledge that you are enough! For example, you might say something like, "I'm really tired today so I'm going to honor that," or "I am worthy and valuable and I deserve to just sit for a little bit."

We need to stop telling ourselves we suck. We are very good at telling ourselves what we are doing is not enough *exactly because* we are so accustomed to doing so much, whether we are in corporate America, or we're an entrepreneur, or we're a stay-at-home mom. No matter what you do, if you're doing it from a place that says, "I am not enough," you are never going to feel happy and you are never going to feel whole.

We as women tend to get uncomfortable when others try to help us, give us compliments, or acknowledge our successes. Why is that? It's because we are often not good *receivers*. Women are naturally so many beautiful things: nurturers, protectors, natural born leaders, and strong. So if this is all true why can't we receive? Women are also extremely hard on themselves by nature. We tend to be self-critical and if we feel intimidated we don't always let our natural light shine bright.

It took me years of patience, practice, and positive self-talk to learn how to be a good receiver, to realize that I have value and worth and that when someone gives me a compliment or acknowledges my skills, talents, or work, that I deserve to feel proud and allow myself to receive the love *freely*.

A great trick I discovered that helps us receive is to ask, "Really?" after the compliment or kindness is given us. The person often then showers you with more compliments and praise! Bonus! It's also a comfortable way to begin to receive more freely. It works! You should try it! There is a movement afoot, teaching women to be supportive of each other, teaching them not to be insecure or intimidated by others' success. We're always or very often comparing ourselves to others. What is that? YOU are the only one that decides how you measure up and it's really only in relation to where YOU want to be in this life. It has nothing to do with others and their success or goals.

I want to help women realize their *beautiful brilliance* at every stage of their lives. I want you to embrace your inner badass! It doesn't matter if we're talking career, body image, self worth, relationships, or goals—I want YOU to own and embrace all of it! No more comparing, as it's a big, fat waste of your time! Only more receiving. Deal?

If you lack in self-love the secret is to practice. Do this exercise with me, it will improve your self-love. Start by choosing five of the following sayings, or write down five things you would like to hear someone you love say, such as:

I am strong.

I am healthy.

I am full of joy.

I am powerful.

I am kind.

I am fearless.

I am safe.

I am enough.

I am worthy.

I am beautiful.

I am smart.

I am amazing.

I am a warrior.

Once you've chosen or invented five sayings, write them down and keep them on a mirror or a night stand. You could also put them on your cell phone. I'd like you to say them every morning before your feet hit the floor and every night before your head hits the pillow. Do this for 30 days and let me know how you feel. I guarantee, you will not only begin to feel better about yourself but you will come to believe these things to be true about you! *They are already true*, you just might need to be reminded or empowered by this positive daily practice.

Listen to your own needs.

Make time for quiet.

Start a daily positive practice of planning out your week to include taking care of yourself. For me, I started going to acupuncture, and acupuncture can be really expensive so I've found that there is *community acupuncture* for a fraction of the cost. You can receive massage from students at a discount, so try something new and different just for YOU! You can go to these salt rooms today, where you sit and you breathe in the healthy salts and relieve stress. Or try some energy work such as EFT (emotional freedom technique), tapping, visualization, or a Reiki treatment. You could even put on your sneakers and take a walk. Whatever you decide to do, it's about trying to clear your mind—acknowledge your thoughts and just release them.

Set a goal such as "I'm going to go through my whole day and I'm not going to say anything critical to myself. I will give negative energy no power! *I am bigger than you* (meaning the negative energy)! *I am stronger than you! You are not worthy of my time or attention!"*

In my programs I give girls and women strategies, such as when you find yourself about to say something not so nice to yourself, just stop. And don't beat yourself up if you slip, like "Oh, shoot, I did that again!" No, just say to yourself, "I see you, negative thought, I acknowledge you, and I am not going to give you any value. I know you're trying to creep in, little, nasty thought! But I'm bigger than you! I am more powerful than you."

These things might even sound weird, but it's all of these little things I've found to do along the way that have given me a lot of peace and clarity, a lot of *ahh*. So I tell people to use these daily, loving thoughts. "I am a rock star," for example. If you say that enough to yourself you will believe it. I myself had more negative self-talk going on than I even realized. It was when I slowed down and began to acknowledge it that I was able to stop it. Otherwise negative energy will eat you from the inside-out.

The best way to show yourself BIG LOVE is to schedule your own "self care" time. It might be something as simple as sitting quietly, reading a book, or walking in nature. Maybe it's taking a drive, meditating, doing energy work, scheduling a massage or healing treatment. The key is to create time and space for you to just *be* and then honor that time. It's okay to give yourself the morning off once in a while, to say, "I don't know *what* I'm going to do today. Maybe I'll just go for a drive." Here in New England in the fall, it's really nice to just go for a drive because of the beautiful colors. Go be in nature, nature is so therapeutic. Find a lake and watch the ducks. In the winter, bundle up with mittens and a hat, and go outside. If we tell ourselves, "It's yucky outside. This is going to be *cold*, this is going to be miserable," it will be! But we can instead say, "You know what? I am going to *conquer* my day. I'm going to bundle up and touch the snow and act like a kid." Sometimes self-love is letting yourself be at *play*. Adults forget how. Play catch with your kid or go play tennis. Think of something you loved when you were younger that maybe you haven't done in a really long time, and go do that.

You and those you love deserve the choices you make to be made from a place of deep meaning and self-love, and we deserve to feel good along the way.

Your happiness is a *choice*!

"Pain is pain, but suffering is the
avoidance of pain. When we avoid the
pain and we don't move through or heal
it, we just continue to suffer."

—Erin Mahoney

{ 2 } The Power of Sitting in the Pain

———— ∞ ————

How long do you feel you need to suffer? In my classes, when we talk about sitting in the pain, I ask questions such as "How long has the pain been there? Do *we allow* this pain to be part of our life, and if so for how long?" When I think about the subject, for myself, I have to ask "What are some of the most painful areas for me as well as others?" The answers are usually grieving and loss, whether loss through a death, divorce, separation, abandonment, or childhood trauma. There can also be pain from things that happen in our careers.

We want to be at a certain place or level, we want to get joy out of our careers, and if we're not getting that, those can be painful things too. There's pain in personal failure. I know as an entrepreneur, I've put plans together and thought, "Oh, this is going to be dynamite!" and then it doesn't go at all as I expected. Whatever the source, those failures are actually huge, learning opportunities. However, before we see the opportunity we must feel the pain.

In my other books I talk about my own mom and how she passed away very suddenly and unexpectedly because of an aneurysm in her brain 17 years ago. The greatest lessons I now offer others and the strength I find today come from the woman that she was. They come from how she raised us. The other half of me—and the rest of the story of my life—is about my dad. It's a story I've never told, until now.

My parents divorced when I was two and my sister was five, and I don't have a relationship with my dad today. We push a lot of things aside that we don't want to think about, or we compartmentalize them, but because of my own personal development, energy work, and the different things that I practice, I've been able to forgive my dad and his shortcomings and allow myself to realize that my relationship with him *had very little to do with me*. I'm so happy today, and I'm good with the situation, but I never would have arrived in this peaceful place without sitting in the pain. It was very painful on many different levels at many different times in my life. It truly doesn't hurt anymore because I gave it the time and understanding it required of me to move forward in a positive way.

Before they split, I remember my parents yelling at each other on one occasion when they still lived in the house together. It was when they used to have the old Coke bottles. My mom came in with a bag of groceries. She and my dad were having a conflict, yelling at each other, my sister and I were small. A bag broke. Grapefruits and oranges went everywhere, all over the kitchen. My sister who was five or six, went running in because that was kind of neat, all of those fruits and colors all over the place, and when she did, my dad was upset with my mom and he took one of those mini Coke bottles and whipped the bottle at my mother. I remember that noise, the glass, and my mom scooping up my sister and saying to him, "The moment you endanger my children, *we are done.*"

And that's painful. I remember moments of my mom's pain, of her making difficult decisions, and probably wondering, "How am I going to take care of these little girls on my own?" But even when I was 12, I still wanted my parents to get back together. I wanted my *family together.* My dad used to say he was going to take us to the Cape (we used to do family vacations down on Cape Cod). I remember my mom getting us ready. She packed our stuff and put it at the screen door. We waited and we waited. "Maybe he's not coming," my mom said. I was always the last one at the screen door. I remember feeling like I had waited for hours, but was sure he was still going to come. *Certainly he would call if something happened. Is he not okay? Why would he do that, just not show up?*

I was living in a house with a mom who was so caring and so reliable, and on the other side, this other parent, this other part of me, and he was so *not present*, so not thoughtful of his little girl's feelings. That situation always ended the same way, with my mom peeling me off of the screen door, saying, "He's not coming."

As an adult I needed to sit in that pain. I didn't want to think about it back then. I was still blaming myself—*Why didn't he love me? Why are my sister and I not enough?* By sitting in the pain, by confronting it, I finally realized those were all *his* issues to sort out, they had very little to do with two little girls who wanted more than anything to be a part of their dad's life. Did you know that you can sit in the pain and ultimately feel better? It's the *avoidance* of the pain that makes you suffer!

We hear all the time how people don't talk to family members, friends, or co-workers, because they had some kind of a falling out or disagreement. By sitting in that pain you realize what a powerful being you are. You realize that you can only be responsible for *your* actions and *your* thoughts. So with that, I—just like you—got to make a decision: "What do I want this to feel like to me? Where do I want to go from here?"

We get to decide. That's what sitting in that space and acknowledging all of that pain helped me to realize, helped me to get to that better place of, "I know what I want this to feel and look like to me. How long do I punish myself, or others? How long do I punish him because he wasn't a great dad?" I know my grandfather wasn't a warm, fuzzy person, so maybe my dad couldn't deal with his own pain, or didn't know how to be a loving father. I realized I don't have to be angry at another person just because they don't express their emotions or they don't behave in a way that I would like them to. It doesn't have to hurt me and it also doesn't need to make me bitter.

People are different and they process their emotions differently. Once we realize that, acknowledge it, and even respect it, we can move through more easily and in a way that serves us. We can let go, we can let other people off the hook, with compassion and understanding, and with *forgiveness*. And for me and my dad, I don't have to analyze it anymore.

Sitting in the pain is one of the six tools, one of the six powers. We have to ask ourselves in any situation, "Is this serving me in a positive way? Do I feel like I need to hold on to it? I don't need to fix it, it's *fixed*. It is what it is. And it doesn't have to be painful."

You gain strength, courage, and confidence by every experience in which you really stop to look fear in the face. You are able to say to yourself, "I lived through this horror. I can take the next thing that comes along. Fear is not real and I've got this!"

Philosopher Friedrich Nietzsche said "That which does not kill us makes us stronger," and he was right, it does, but only if we sit with it and then *decide to* move through it. Practice letting yourself off the hook and releasing the pain! You have held onto it long enough. Is it serving you? If so, in what way? How might you show up in a more loving way to let go of this pain?

My story is an example of the *power* of sitting in the pain, and it leads right into the Power of Forgiveness. We get to choose if we want to be bitter or angry. We get to choose if we want to be happy and move on!

I choose *happy* and movin' on!

"You are the only one keeping YOU on the hook! Let yourself off the hook already!"

—Erin Mahoney

{ 3 } The Power of Forgiveness

---- &ი ----

Forgiveness is what sets you *free.* It can set other people free, too. If I had not been able to forgive myself and change my behavior *before* my kids didn't want me to tuck them in anymore, or if I had not been able to forgive my father, I would be stuck in resentment and anger at both myself and my dad. I have no resentment. I am not angry, and I am certainly not *stuck*! I have moved on, and the life I have been able to create and lead since practicing these powers has been rich, free, and fulfilling. Life is not always perfect but it's pretty damn good and I know it's only the beginning! You have the power to make your life pretty darn good, too!

I have learned that you can't get to forgiving yourself without loving yourself first. Sometimes we need to acknowledge we might not be showing ourselves the love we deserve. You need to ask yourself, "Am I loving *me* enough? Am I loving me at all? How can I show myself the love?" You may need to reprogram your brain to get into a positive vibe if you have been existing in a negative vibe. It will take practice, dedication, and focus. You need to *want* to make change for the better and then *do the work*!

We all make mistakes. Did you know that no one else is keeping track of your mistakes? If they are, they are not your people! That simple. We're the only ones that keep us on the hook—the only one that is keeping *you* on the hook is *you*. Sometimes we don't show up to our lives or situations as our best selves. It's okay, we are human and can't always be "on." We can, however acknowledge mistakes, vow to do better in the future, and move on. Simple, right? That is forgiveness, self-love, and freedom in the most beautiful form.

We all know people who tell themselves they stink all the time. They're not getting anything they want out of life because it all starts from that place of "I am not enough." When and where does that happen? When do we start to tell ourselves we're not enough? As children? From our parents?

Does it even matter?

We can't forgive others who have caused us pain until we have exercised the power of sitting in the pain, enough to decide to move on.

Set yourself FREE!

You get to *choose* to let go of pain, to choose to stop carrying it around. And that's what the power of forgiveness does.

And *why* don't we quickly forgive ourselves or others? Is it a past family pattern, past traumas? Do we "enjoy" wallowing in self-pity? Does that serve us or others? No, it only holds us back. Again, forgiveness is a powerful way to start moving *forward*.

When you *practice* forgiveness of yourself and of others, *you* begin to heal. You begin to break old patterns. You start to see that *you* deserve happiness, we all do. Tell yourself over and over, "I will forgive myself, I *am* enough, I will do my best and my best is always good enough. Although I have pain, fear, and anger, I am still a *rock star*. I will forgive because *I am enough*. I will forgive *me*. I will release the fear, pain, and anger and I will because I *am enough*. I love myself deeply and completely." Now say that all over again and continue to say it until it begins to feel good. Practice self-forgiveness with NO GUILT. This takes practice but as you'll see, it can be done! Begin to practice forgiving others, too.

Forgiveness brings back and helps you hold a tremendous amount of power.

Even in your darkest, weakest moments, you are strong, worthy, and beautiful! So let yourself and those you love but have not forgiven yet, *out of jail!*

We have been there way too long.

"If you want to travel fast, go alone. If you want to travel far, go together."

—African proverb of the N'gambai people

{ 4 } The Power of Navigating Relationships

——— ∞ ———

What are our most meaningful relationships? Family? Children? Spouses? Partners? Siblings? Friends? And what are the most difficult relationships we have? Family? Children? Spouses? Partners? Siblings? Friends?

Get the point?

Should relationships be built on compassion and love? Should relationships serve *both* parties?

Yes, yes, absolutely yes!

Relationships come in many different forms. Their depths vary and they are built upon many different qualities. *Only you* can decide what is most important to you. You also get to decide what feels best in a relationship to you. Sometimes we make relationships and life harder than they have to be. I have found that when I keep it simple, have clarity about my relationships, speak my truth, and set realistic expectations and boundaries, the people that I am supposed to have in my life appear and often stay. Others come in and out of our lives at specific times and that's okay. It's actually necessary. Not all people are meant to stay in our lives forever.

Love your relationships when they work. Try not to stress, fix, or force them when they don't, and always come from a place of love and kindness. If you navigate in this way your relationships are sure to flourish!

Know that some relationships will have a start and an ending point and there is sadness in that. At times we might need to have some self-reflection about a relationship. Remember when thinking about past relationships to practice self-love and learn from what comes up. No blame or shame game here, just learning!

One's philosophy is not best expressed in words; it is expressed in the choices one makes. The choices we make are ultimately our own responsibility. That's all we can and should be responsible for. It's important to hold others responsible for their choices without anger, judgment, or fear.

I had to realize in my situation with my dad that he was missing it. He didn't get it. He didn't know me as a person, and he doesn't know how fabulous I am today. He doesn't know how *incredible* his grandsons are. That made me feel sad for him, but it also made me feel strong in the fact that *I* set the boundaries. I was able to be protective of my own feelings and spare my kids the pain of disappointment that I endured for so many years. It has helped me to feel healthy and empowered me to teach that strength and wisdom to others.

Realize that you have to take care of *yourself*, of your own health and happiness.

If someone is missing it or they don't get you and they're not in your vibe, it's on them—and it's okay. Not everybody is going to align with us, whether career, family, friends, or it might simply not be the right *time or space* for that relationship.

Just because a relationship looks a certain way *now* doesn't mean it will look that way forever. Just because you are friends and you've talked to this person every day for the last two years, doesn't mean you're going to talk to them every day for the next two years.

And that's okay.

It doesn't mean you love them less. It doesn't mean they love you less. It doesn't mean there's a conflict. It just means *relationships change.* And you need to navigate in and out of those. People come into our lives for a certain period of time. Some people come into our lives for eternity.

Sometimes we hold on so tightly to something we think should last forever, that we're actually blocking ourselves from another, new, more beautiful relationship. I've found that if you let the wrong people take up space in your life, you might be blocking other people from coming in, people who really get you. It's not good for us to hold on to negative energy, so we need to accept people as they are, where they are, and do what feels most healthy to us, and always come from that place of love and kindness if we can.

In navigating relationships I ask the Universe, "What does this relationship mean? Does this relationship fill something that is mutually beneficial?" There is nothing wrong with saying that any relationship should serve both parties in a positive way.

And isn't that a beautiful thing?

It doesn't matter if it's a career, family, or personal relationship.

Our own view of ourselves plays into this, our own self-worth. If we feel like we're not worthy of more, we punish ourselves, and we sometimes stay in places where it's not good for us. We see others do this all the time: "I'm staying in a job I hate because I need the money." Or we stay in a broken marriage "for the kids." These thoughts and actions come from a place of fear. Do not let fear cloud your judgment. Be fearless, look for solutions, be brave and make change! You deserve to LOVE YOUR LIFE! Fear is not real, fear is the *thought* we create that makes us stuck and makes us miss our lives!

Navigating relationships can be a very sticky proposition, or you can simply decide, "This doesn't have to be sticky." So wash off the glue. Decide, "I'm not going to be stuck. I'm going to be open, with an open heart and open mind." Do what feels good to you and things really do fall into place. It sounds simplistic, but they really do, trust me!

When you are true to yourself, people either melt away or they *show up*. And if they show up, you navigate together, even through the painful moments. Work through the relationships that are valuable to you, and let go of the others.

There's a difference between compassion and love and being a door mat! I can be compassionate and loving, but I get to set the boundaries that you don't get to hurt me anymore. When we practice grace and forgiveness toward others it allows them to be more open and forgiving as well. Everybody wins and relationships grow. It frees everybody up to have good energy, to have good vibes.

Test out your ability to be compassionate and loving. Journal your feelings around holding others' actions from a place of love and kindness especially those that are difficult relationships for you.

And over time, find your tribe!

"No one can make you feel inferior
without your consent."

—Eleanor Roosevelt

{ 5 } The Power of Letting Go

———— ∽ ————

Part of happiness is *letting go* of toxic relationships, of self blame, of these unrealistic expectations we put upon ourselves, and focusing instead on the *positives* we are creating in our lives. After I learned how to *let go* in a way that made me feel free of guilt, shame, or emotions that didn't serve me, I wanted to share what I knew with the world. It is my firm belief that letting go means getting out of *our own way*. It means letting go of negative thoughts and negative self-talk. It means releasing emotions that are harmful to us or make us experience physical tension.

In order to let go you must surrender to the fact that things won't always go perfectly, or as you hoped or planned, but that they are in fact just as they should be at the moment. This means you must stop worrying! Letting go *completely* means you can't worry about your relationships, your family, your job, your career, the traffic, your bills, your health, and everything else in your life. You must literally let go in order to experience true abundance, joy, love, peace, gratitude, and happiness. By practicing the power of letting go, you no longer need to "fix" things, try to control outcomes, or worry about what other people's opinions are.

Can you imagine all the time you'll have when you stop worrying and stop carrying the burden of fixing *everything*? You allow yourself to be you! You begin to love yourself and others more with an openness that is secure and confident.

Do you see how this works?

Letting go almost always follows forgiveness. Let yourself and others off the hook, forgive, let go, and move on. Just like that you get to feel good, and you *deserve* to feel amazing.

Are your relationships or situations serving you in a positive way? If not STOP IT and LET GO!

What do you hang on to and why? Have you been hanging on too long? What do you think that's about?

What's really underneath the hanging on is actually fear, guilt, sadness, and uncertainty. When you let that go, everything underneath goes with it. We are only responsible for our own words, actions and opinions. Don't carry around those of anyone else! Don't allow people to mess with your mojo. You get to choose if someone is going to mess up your vibe.

Take your time, breathe, and have faith that everything will work out, and when possible, *let go!*

We decide how we are going to hold our energy. Waste no more time holding on to things that make you feel angry or sad. Remember, if it's not serving you in a positive way you need to let it go. You then get to give yourself credit for doing the difficult, because many times letting go is difficult. Celebrate *you* and the shifts that *you* are making to let go of situations and relationships that don't serve you. How freeing is that?

"The future belongs to those who believe
in the beauty of their dreams."

—Eleanor Roosevelt

{ 6 } The Power of Goal Setting

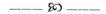

People need to be really careful with goal setting. I didn't always know that. I'm a very goal-oriented person. I love to do vision boards and look at my goals, think about my goals, and review my goals often. There is power in that. However, we also need to realize that it is necessary to allow goals to change and evolve without beating ourselves up in the process. I love teaching people how to see when their goals have shifted or changed and how to embrace that. It's something that encompasses all the powers that we have already discussed. Letting goals change, shift, or letting a particular goal go away altogether can be difficult.

I can help you with that.

Along my Girl Power journey I was working very hard and getting kind of burned out. In addition, there wasn't a lot of income because I was all over the place. I was struggling with my worthiness and I was stuck! Back then I didn't understand the power of slowing down or sitting in the pain so I just kept piling more things onto my plate. It was a hot mess. I added more and more and I joined a multi-level marketing company. Yup, I was sure this was my way to wealth and fulfillment. Holy crap was I wrong!

I set all of these huge goals: I was going to build a big team, get to the "vice presidential" level, and I was going to get that fancy car. I was pretty successful at it. I built a team pretty quickly. I went up through the ranks pretty quickly. But just before the vice-presidential level I realized I wasn't loving my life, and this goal I had set for myself was actually beating the crap out of me.

That was a huge moment for me. What the heck was I doing? What did I really want from my life? What was my passion? Why was I chasing the hustle all the time? Why couldn't I slow the heck down and really figure this out?

In doing this self-evaluation and asking myself those deep, painful questions I realized that in order to figure it out I needed to love myself more, sit in the pain, forgive, and let go. Once I did those things my goals became crystal clear and they had nothing to do with being part of a multi-level marketing company or chasing the hustle. They had everything to do with loving my life, with building my work and relationships in a way that made me feel my best, and with only making decisions from a place of calm, self-love, and deep meaning. No more decisions would be made in the heat of the moment, out of fear or panic.

I realized it's okay sometimes to say, "That's not the goal anymore," and to let go instead of telling myself things like "I stink! I failed. I didn't do what I said I was going to do." I had to learn to say, "This goal is not that important to me anymore, and I have new goals.

So realize *goals change*, and always assess your goals by what is most important to you, what you want your life to look like. For me, I wanted to have *impact*. I wanted to have a positive outcome on others as well as myself. So I needed to love my work, it needed to be in line with my family life and what's most meaningful to me. If your goal sits outside of that you have to re-evaluate.

Set goals for yourself that have *direction*. Know what path you want to take. But also know that those goals and your vision can change and it doesn't have to be a big beat-down. It just means the thing that was really important to you *then* doesn't feel so important to you *now*.

It might be important to let that go and set new goals.

When we are talking about goal setting I always suggest women make a list of what is most important to them and how they will work toward achieving their goals. Ask yourself, "*Why* is this goal important to me?" Imagine how it will feel when you reach the goal. Ask yourself what sacrifices if any you might need to take to make the goal a reality. How do these questions feel to you, and do they bring up any unexpected emotions? Fear? Excitement? Insecurity? Guilt? Pride? By doing this exercise you will gain clarity and have the ability to commit to or eliminate goals you set in the future.

To be happy we have to allow ourselves to have these shifts from time to time. We must be flexible with our own goals as we learn and grow. Have the courage to set big fat goals, and do the work to reach them. Practice self-love, forgiveness, and letting go if necessary for a big fat goal to change. The key is to love yourself through the entire process and know that you have the power and right to change your mind and change your goals at any given time. Your work is to stay positive, speak your truth, and be brave!

"You get to choose what your life is going to feel and look like."

—Erin Mahoney

Energy Work

I'm all about positive vibes. When we raise our vibration, the things that we want come to us. When you exercise *your six powers*, true positive vibes are finally possible. Some call it *integrity*, which means "whole." My friend plays drums and he cracked a cymbal once—we knew because it made a horrible, quiet, gaspy sound whenever he hit it. That's life where one of your six powers are missing. No good vibes, even when you "try" because they're still *forced*. In *Positive Vibes*, we're not after *forced* but *flow*.

Energy work can do wonders in achieving that, and there are a few methods I'd love to share with you right now.

TAPPING

Like acupuncture and acupressure, tapping is a set of techniques which utilize the body's energy meridian points. You can stimulate these meridian points by tapping on them with your fingertips, literally tapping into your body's own energy and healing power. EFT tapping is a combination of ancient Chinese acupressure and modern psychology. Tapping provides relief from chronic pain, emotional problems, disorders, addictions, phobias, post traumatic stress disorder (PTSD), and physical diseases[1]. Your body is more powerful than you can imagine, filled with life, energy, and a compelling ability for self-healing. With tapping, you can take control of that power. Tapping is easy to learn and can move you into a positive place in a very short period of time. Give it a try!

---

[1] www.thetappingsolution.com

For more about tapping and for a few tapping meditations check out www.thetappingsolution.com.

MEDITATION

Meditation is defined as a state of deep peace when the mind becomes calm and silent. Not an easy place for many of us to find in our over-scheduled and often overwhelming lives. Meditation takes practice but with patience it is possible to achieve a calm, peaceful state. Setting your *intention* to *be still* is half the battle. Once you set your intention and create the time and space for yourself you can "drop in" to the practice of meditating.

When I work with clients or classrooms of ladies I remind them throughout our guided meditation that things are just right, just as they are in your meditation practice. Some days it's harder to find the quiet. Some days it doesn't show up at all, and other days you arrive in stillness very quickly. The key is to acknowledge the thoughts as they come into your mind and release them without judgment or attachment. Be gentle and kind to yourself as you learn this new way of taking care of yourself.

"Love and kindness" meditations are one of my favorites. Let's try one! Say to yourself:

May I be safe.

May I be free from harm.

May I be peaceful and full of joy.

May I be full of love and kindness.

Repeating these statements can calm your energy. They're positive affirmations, but done in a very meditative state when you're conscious but relaxed and present. I'll ask students to then say these things to themselves:

May I be safe.

May I be peaceful.

May I be full of joy.

May I be free from stress.

May I be free from anxiety.

May I treat myself well today.

You can also work gratitude into these meditations.

VISUALIZATION

I love the power of visualization. It's easy to teach and is a powerful tool for gaining mindfulness. It's a healthy way to bring positive energy into your mind, body, and spirit. You can use visualization in many ways. One of the ways I like to use it with students is to have them think of a time they experienced pain, then put that as far away as they can in their minds, sitting quietly, talking through it. I guide them with questions like, "How does that feel to you? What do you see?" It's about helping women gain a heightened awareness and drop into their space and bodies.

Then of course, the other visualization is to have people think of those things that make them *happy* and full of joy, doing comparisons, trying to think of happy things that are far away from you and bringing them closer. If it's something that makes you uncomfortable and we try to bring it closer, it might bring up feelings of fear and insecurity. Guidance during visualization helps with a feeling of safety, comfort, and calm.

BREATHING

Working with the breath is a wonderful way to create calm in your body, mind, and spirit. I teach how to give credit to the breath. Sometimes it's just a matter of sitting and connecting with your breath, talking about how the breath feels as it starts in your belly, as the chest then rises as it moves through your neck, and then as you exhale, releasing negative energy. Taking deep, slow breaths in will help you create clarity and calm in your energy.

I teach being *grateful* for the breath. The breath is something that shows up for us, morning, noon, and night. It asks nothing of us, and we don't ever pay attention to it. We only pay attention to it when we lose one, and then we're in trouble. That's always a very grounding practice, to appreciate the breath. When we feel overwhelmed, we can always find a clear state of mind knowing we have that, that we have the breath and a place of gratitude and appreciation

Something as simple as connecting to the breath can bring a state of great calm, stillness, and comfort. *Love* the breath and slow down to acknowledge and enjoy it often!

YOGA

I like to do slow-movement yoga when I'm in an energy work mindset. No quick movements—just slow, lengthening and strengthening, mindful movements. We bring an awareness to the body and love it just the way it is in this moment. Feel yourself getting settled into the space by grounding your feet to the earth and allowing your head to float through the sky, lengthening your spine and coming in contact with the breath. Allow yourself to be completely relaxed. At times that is not possible but with continued focus and determination it will come.

Appreciate whatever the practice brings each time you do it and celebrate your efforts. It's about where you *are*—not about where you are going! Try to bring awareness to your shoulders and pull them up and back. With stress or unhappiness we often times round them forward. Be mindful of your posture. Be long and tall, chest out and open. Your body is soft but strong with no resistance.

Yoga will nourish you in so many ways so give it a try!

SLOWING DOWN

It's okay to slow down once n a while. It's actually really good for you! Sometimes the minute we stop we tell ourselves we're lazy, we're not motivated, we should be doing more—and *that's bullshit!* Those are just broken recordings in our heads. Realize that it's fairly impossible to be present if we never slow down, and there's a cost to never letting ourselves slow down.

There are so many ways we can find to slow down, we're bound to like or love a few, whether it's reflexology, massage, acupuncture, or any of the modalities I've mentioned. Be open-minded and try new things. Find what works for you to slow down, be present and unwind. You might find something that really serves you.

Things you may have been holding on to for years will begin to feel lighter and less important. They will eventually melt away if they are not serving you in a positive way. I know because I have experienced it. Try some or all of these techniques or find your own. Give them each a chance. Find what works for you, and repeat as often as you like. Connect with me, and we'll do even more.

"Things are about to get really good.

Rock the day!"

—Erin Mahoney

Conclusion: Positive Vibes

———— ∽ ————

When I was younger, I ran track in high school. At the time, my dad had remarried and my oldest step-brother was an incredible runner. He was a senior when I was a freshman. I was running winter track for the first time, and although I was good at the sport I was nervous and lacked confidence. I remember this one particular track meet that I was running in after school but my brother wasn't able to be there. We talked about my nervousness the night before. The day began like any other day and I packed up my track gear and books and went off to school. When it came time for me to get ready for the meet I found a note tucked into one of my track sneakers.

This note clearly had a lasting impact on me. I was 14 years old when I found it and I have kept it all of these years. I remember pulling it out of my sneaker and reading it like it was yesterday. It said, "Success is not a result of spontaneous combustion. You must set yourself on fire." I love that quote (It's by Arnold H. Glasow). It's so powerful, and I have called upon this memory many times in my life. When I first read the quote I instantly thought, "Yes, that's exactly what I will do!" I ran my butt off that day and placed second in the 200-meter sprint as a freshman. I will never forget it or that note!

I "set myself on fire," in a sense, with my Girl Power Go mission to empower girls and women everywhere through massive action and positive thoughts. The importance and value of the work fuels me. I will never quit. I will never give up. I want to inspire and support women by spreading positive vibes. I will continue to ignite the fire and watch it spread. I want to have a lasting impact on all women that read this book just as that note had a lasting impact on me.

My vision is for you to set yourself aflame with all that you love, all that's important to you, and all that makes you feel your very best! I want you to have fun on your journey. Know that it's impossible to make the "wrong" choice along the way. Our choices bring us to where we need to go and they always teach us something. Keep learning, as you move through and forward.

Splurge! Use *your* six powers to achieve and enjoy positive vibes, and spread the word!

The Power of Self-Love

The Power of Sitting in the Pain

The Power of Forgiveness

The Power of Navigating Relationships

The Power of Letting Go

The Power of Goal Setting

~

In closing, below you will find my Things I Love About Me worksheet I use in many of my women's classes. I have placed a printable copy for you at www.GirlPowerGo.com if you like. Fill this out and know that it may change at different times, depending on when you use it. It's designed as a tool to help you with self-love and to bring clarity to the things that make you feel your best, with things that you might want to do more often because feeling your best IS THE GOAL, right? and YOU DESERVE THAT!

THINGS I LOVE ABOUT ME

Developing Strong Women

Write down five *positive* I AM statements you would not normally say to yourself:

1. "I am _____"

2. "I am _____"

3. "I am _____"

4. "I am _____"

5. "I am _____"

Say the above I AM statements every night before your head hits the pillow and every morning before your feet hit the floor.

Now fill in the following additional statements about YOU:

I love that I am

_____

I feel strong when

_____

I feel proud when I

_____

I love myself when

_____

I feel AMAZING when

_____

Remember that it takes practice and patience but YOU ARE WORTH THE EFFORT! Change takes time so be good to _you_ in the meantime.

You are AMAZING and SPECIAL just the way you are, TODAY! The work you are doing is so that YOU can learn to CELEBRATE YOU and live your very BEST LIFE!

And YOU deserve that!

With Love,

Erin

Next Steps

————— 🙰 —————

Know that this journey for you is just beginning and life is a work in progress. My hope is that you will continue to practice all that you have learned and I want you to remain in my "web of love" by staying connected to me and Girl Power Go. Visit and subscribe to our website:

www.GirlPowerGo.com

to hear about live and online events, classes and workshops, or do one-on-one work with me where we will dive deeper and focus on YOU!

I can't wait to see where your journey will take you!

About the Author

ERIN C. MAHONEY

CEO & Founder of Girl Power Go

ERIN HAS OVER 29 years of experience in the health and fitness industry since serving in the United States Air Force. She is the best-selling author of the Girl Power books that explain and accompany the Girl Power program: the *Girl Power Guidebook* for parents and instructors, and the *Girl Power Journal* for girls. She is a motivational speaker and empowerment expert. Erin is a certified personal trainer and group fitness instructor with specialized certifications in yoga and kickboxing. Erin studied meditation, relaxation, and stress reduction at the Center of Mindfulness at the University of Massachusetts Medical Center and is the founder and creator of Girl Power Go, the empowerment company that is on a mission to empower girls and women everywhere! Erin recently published her third book, *Positive Vibes for Women*. When not speaking, training, signing books, or at Gillette Stadium watching her New England Patriots win, Erin is at home in Massachusetts raising her two sons with her husband.

Girl Power Books

THE GIRL POWER GUIDEBOOK,
together with the Girl Power Journal give
you all you need to deliver and get the
maximum out of the empowerment
program for girls between the ages of 8
and 13 taking the U.S. by storm! In this
life-changing course that includes life
skills, fitness, positive thinking, creativity
and fun, girls get excited about being

strong, self-confident, independent and healthy, giving them the tools they need to make good decisions in our ever demanding society.

THE GIRL POWER JOURNAL is the beautifully illustrated and interactive book that empowers young girls between the ages of 8 and 13 to discover themselves as powerful, smart, happy, and amazing! This is the original and complete program founded by Erin C. Mahoney that is taking the U.S. by storm, and which is now available everywhere in published book form! In this life-changing course that includes life skills, fitness, positive thinking, creativity and fun, girls get excited about being strong, self-confident, independent and healthy, giving them the tools they need to make good decisions in our ever demanding society. Also available for parents and instructors is the GIRL POWER GUIDEBOOK to assist in delivery of the Girl Power program.

Recommended Reading

———— 🙢 ————

The Gifts of Imperfection, Daring Greatly and Rising Strong by Brene Brown

Wherever You Go, There You Are: Mindfulness Meditation in Everyday Life by John Kabat-Zinn

What I Know for Sure by Oprah Winfrey

The Greatness Guide: 101 Lessons for Making What's Good at Work and in Life Even Better by Robin Sharma

The Four Agreements by Don Miquel Ruiz

A Short Guide to a Happy Life by Anna Quindlen

"That which does not kill us makes us stronger."

—Friedrich Nietzsche

"Dreams really do come true!"

—Erin Mahoney

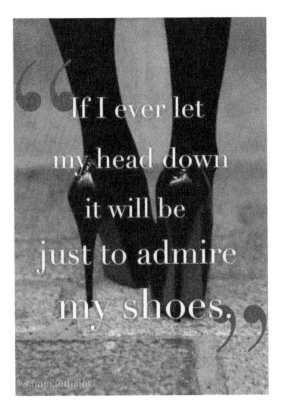

If I ever let my head down it will be just to admire my shoes.

@samanthaow

"Never quit on YOU or your dreams!

—Erin Mahoney

Image Credits

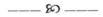

COVER: "Young Woman Standing in Field and Throwing Arms Up" by bholland via www.istockphoto.com

EPIGRAPH: "Cherry Blossom" by Ludovic Bertron [CC BY 2.0], via Wikimedia Commons

THE POWER OF YOU: "Katy" by Kelly Chester

{ 1 } THE POWER OF SELF-LOVE: "Hermosa mujer usando ropa de invierno" by CoffeeAndMilk via www.istockphoto.com

{ 2 } THE POWER OF SITTING IN THE PAIN: "On the Hook and Freedom" via https://www.youtube.com/watch?v=_nGQCAIMVI0

{ 3 } THE POWER OF FORGIVENESS: "Butterfly Chains" via http://filonoi.gr/2013/06/27/f-dixos-biasynh/

{ 4 } THE POWER OF NAVIGATING RELATIONSHIPS: "Smiling Women" by dolgachov via www.canstockphoto.com

{ 5 } THE POWER OF LETTING GO: "Blue Eagle Hd Wallpaper" via http://wallpapers-kid.com/blue-eagle-hd-wallpaper/blue-eagle-hd-wallpaper.htm

{ 6 } THE POWER OF GOAL SETTING: Image of Author, "Resistance" by the Author

ENERGY WORK: "3638868545_3e65a7f849_s" via www.flickr.com

POSITIVE VIBES: "Good Vibes" by ArtsyBee via www.pixabay.com

ABOUT THE AUTHOR: *Photo of Author: Makeup, Hair & Photography by Beauty PaRLR and RLR Studio*

"GRLPWR" license plate by the Author: "Shoes" via www.pinterest.co.kr

"Shoes" via
https://www.pinterest.com/pin/370772981802225888/

CPSIA information can be obtained
at www.ICGtesting.com
Printed in the USA
BVOW11s1702300817
493400BV00006B/19/P

9 780998 889757